NFL Teams

New York Jets

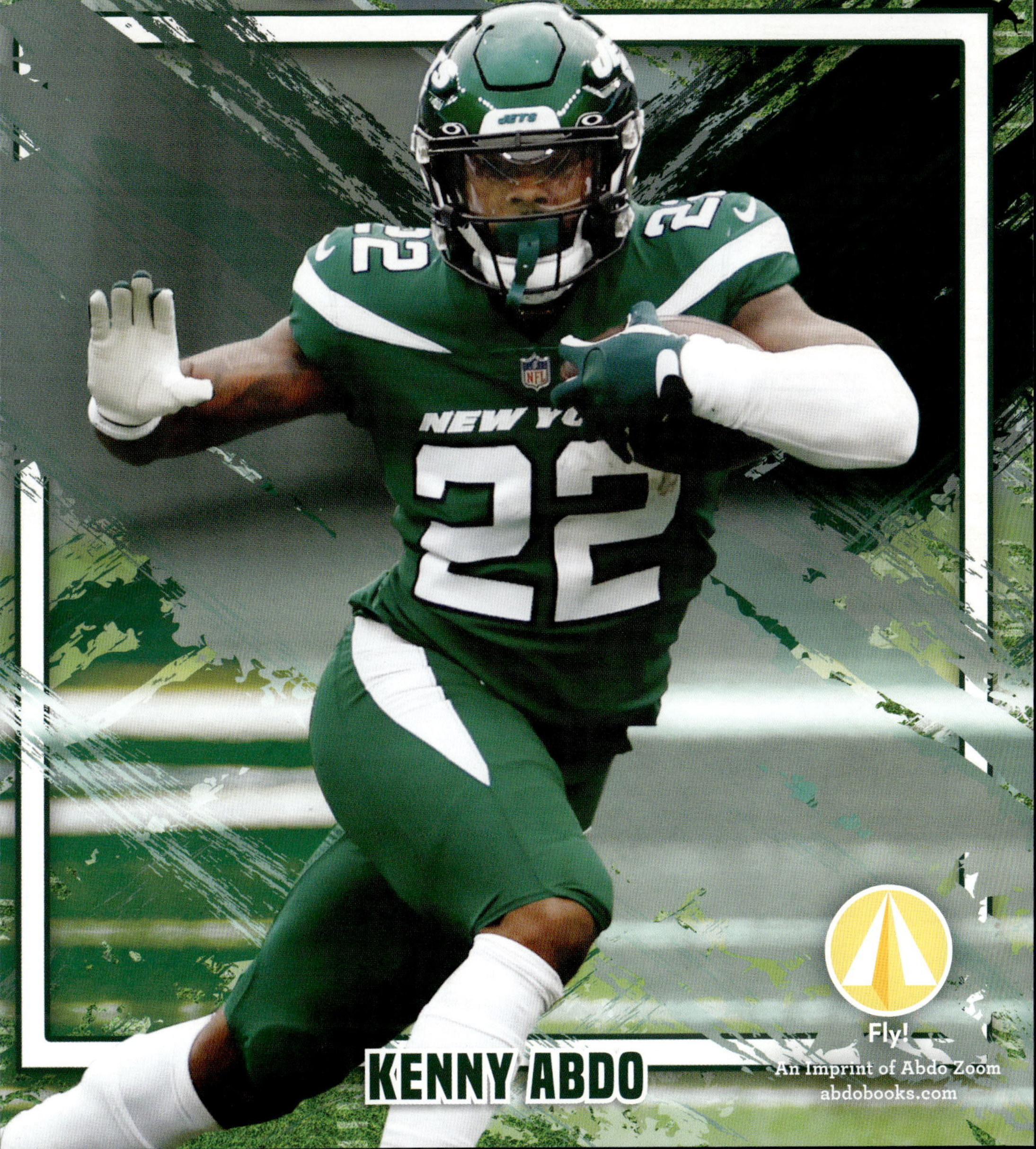

Kenny Abdo

Fly!
An Imprint of Abdo Zoom
abdobooks.com

abdobooks.com

Published by Abdo Zoom, a division of ABDO, P.O. Box 398166, Minneapolis, Minnesota 55439.

Printed in China.
052021
092021

THIS BOOK CONTAINS RECYCLED MATERIALS

Photo Credits: Alamy, AP Images, Getty Images, iStock, Shutterstock PREMIER
Production Contributors: Kenny Abdo, Jennie Forsberg, Grace Hansen
Design Contributors: Candice Keimig, Neil Klinepier

Library of Congress Control Number: 2020919727

Publisher's Cataloging-in-Publication Data

Names: Abdo, Kenny, author.
Title: New York Jets / by Kenny Abdo
Description: Minneapolis, Minnesota : Abdo Zoom, 2022 | Series: NFL teams | Includes online resources and index.
Identifiers: ISBN 9781098224752 (lib. bdg.) | ISBN 9781098225698 (ebook) | ISBN 9781098226169 (Read-to-Me ebook)
Subjects: LCSH: New York Jets (Football team)--Juvenile literature. | National Football League--Juvenile literature. | Football teams--Juvenile literature. | American football--Juvenile literature. | Professional sports--Juvenile literature.
Classification: DDC 796.33264--dc23

TABLE OF CONTENTS

New York Jets 4

Kick Off 8

Team Recaps 14

Hall of Fame 24

Glossary 30

Online Resources 31

Index 32

NEW YORK JETS

Representing the "Big Apple" for more than 60 years, the New York Jets fly high in NFL history.

With a **Super Bowl** victory and many trips to the playoffs, the Jets have taken its fans to soaring heights.

JETS

KICK OFF

The Jets started playing in 1960. At first, they were known as the Titans. New owners took over in 1963. They changed the team name to the Jets.

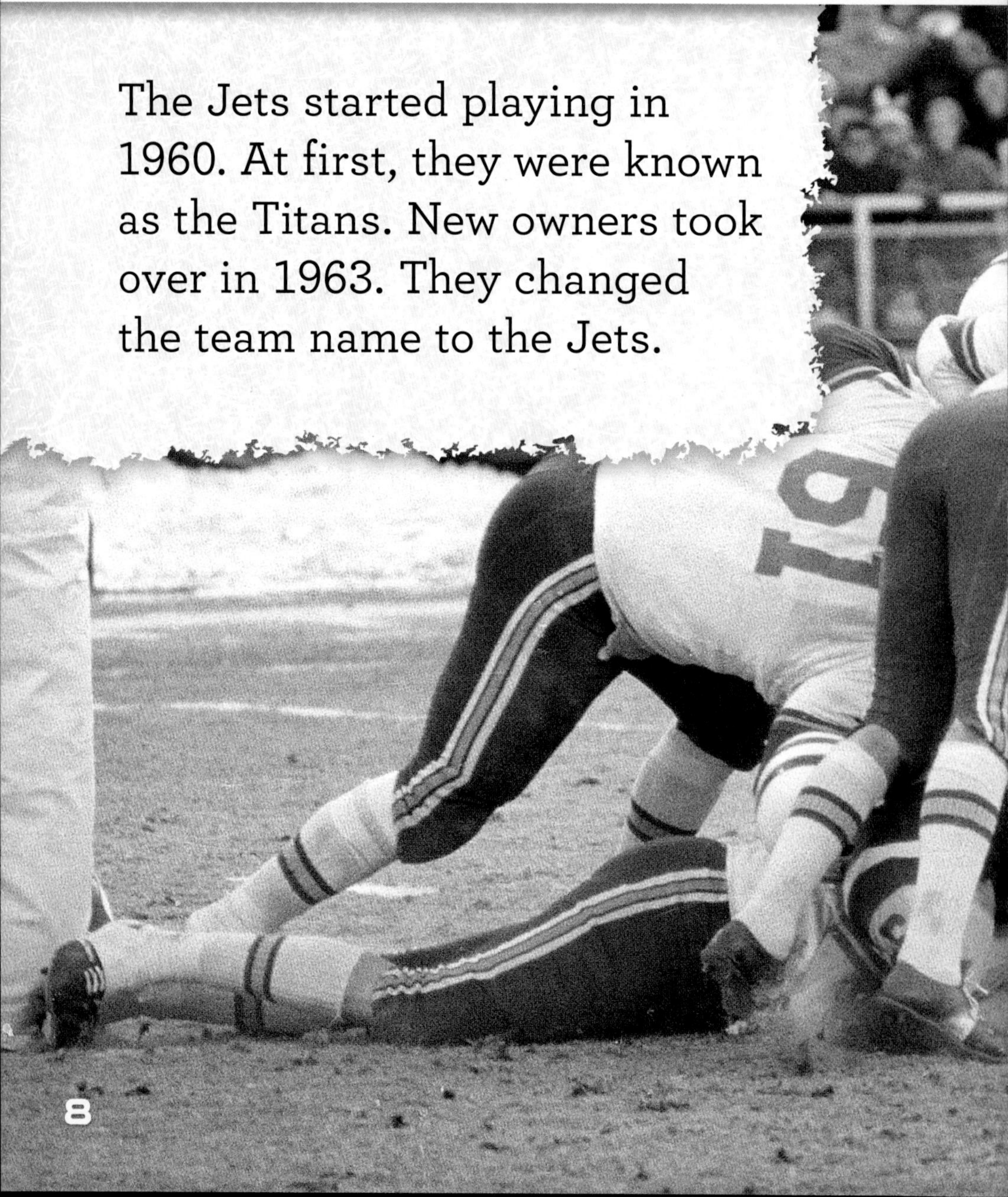

41

The Jets got their name for the location of their new stadium, which sat between New York's two biggest airports. The owners hired Weeb Ewbank as head coach and signed **quarterback** Joe Namath soon after.

All of the decisions paid off. Following the 1968 season, the Jets made it to **Super Bowl** III. In what is thought to be one of the greatest upsets in NFL history, the Jets beat the Baltimore Colts 16–7.

TEAM RECAPS

The Jets did not see the playoffs from 1970 to 1980. They finally made it to a playoff game following the 1981 season. In a sad turn, they lost to the Buffalo Bills 31–27.

The Monday Night Miracle took place on October 23, 2000, at Giants Stadium. The Jets scored a whopping 30 points against the Dolphins in the fourth quarter, sending the game into **overtime**. The Jets came out on top 40–37.

Brett Favre served as the Jets' QB for one season in 2008. In a game against the Arizona Cardinals, he threw six touchdown passes, a career-high for Favre.

The Jets hired head coach Adam Gase in 2019. The team finished with a 7–9 record. Safety Jamal Adams was selected for the Pro Bowl for the third year in a row!

PRO BOWL
33
JETS
NFL

The 2020 season ended with a grim 2–14 record. It was the team's worst since 1996. The Jets let Gase go after just one season. Hopefully, the Jets will fly higher in future seasons.

HALL OF FAME

QB Joe Namath took the Jets to their only **Super Bowl**. He was named the game's **MVP**. When Namath retired, he had passed for 27,663 career yards.

Namath was **inducted** into the Pro Football Hall of Fame in 1985.

Wide receiver Don Maynard was the first player **drafted** to the Jets. In his first year, he had an incredible 72 catches for 1,265 yards. Maynard helped the Jets go to and win **Super Bowl** III! He was **inducted** into the Pro Football Hall of fame in 1987.

JETS
13

Running back Curtis Martin joined the Jets in 1998. He rushed for more than 1,000 yards in each season except for one. That was 10,302 yards as a Jet. Martin was **inducted** into the Pro Football Hall of Fame in 2012.

GLOSSARY

draft – a process in sports to assign athletes to a certain team.

induct – to admit someone as a member of an organization.

MVP – short for "most valuable player," an award given in sports to a player who has performed the best in a game or series.

overtime – additional minutes added to a tied-up game giving each team a chance to win.

quarterback (QB) – the player on the offensive team that directs teammates in their play.

sack – when a quarterback is tackled behind the line of scrimmage while still in possession of the ball.

Super Bowl – the NFL championship game, played once a year.

ONLINE RESOURCES

Booklinks
NONFICTION NETWORK
FREE! ONLINE NONFICTION RESOURCES

To learn more about the New York Jets, please visit abdobooklinks.com or scan this QR code. These links are routinely monitored and updated to provide the most current information available.

INDEX

Adams, Jamal 20

Bills (team) 15

Cardinals (team) 18

Colts (team) 12

Dolphins (team) 17

Ewbank, Weeb 10

Favre, Brett 18

Gase, Adam 20, 22

Martin, Curtis 29

Maynard, Don 26

Namath, Joe 10, 24, 25

Super Bowl 12, 24